AKIBA-SCHECHTER JEWISH DAY SCHOOL
5235 S. Cornell Ave.
Chicago, Illinois 60615-4211

Trading

The earliest traders probably used
rivers as highways on which to
travel to sell their wares. These
waterborne traders in Bangkok
still find business by the riverside.

WAYS OF LIFE

Trading

BY BRIAN WILLIAMS

Illustrated by Bernard Robinson

RSVP

RAINTREE STECK-VAUGHN
PUBLISHERS
The Steck-Vaughn Company

Austin, Texas

Published by Raintree Steck-Vaughn Publishers, an imprint of Steck-Vaughn Company

Designed and produced by AS Publishing

Library of Congress Cataloging-in-Publication Data
Williams, Brian, 1943–
    Trading / by Brian Williams ; illustrated by Bernard Robinson.
      p.   cm. — (Ways of life)
    Includes index.
    Summary: Examines the various ways people have exchanged goods and services around the world from the early days of human history to modern times.
    ISBN 0-8114-4787-1
    1. Commerce—History—Juvenile literature.   [1. Commerce—History.]   I. Robinson, Bernard, 1930–   ill.   II. Title.   III. Series.
HE353.W49   1993
380.1—dc20   92-27031
                                           CIP AC

Typeset by Tom Fenton Studio, Neptune, NJ
Printed in Italy by L.E.G.O. s.p.a., Vicenza
Bound in the United States by Lake Book, Melrose Park, IL

1 2 3 4 5 6 7 8 9 0 LB 98 97 96 95 94 93

Cover credits: Hong Kong Tourist Board (center), Hutchison Library

Picture credits: Michael Holford 25; Honda 36; Hong Kong Tourist Board 6/7; Hulton Deutsch Collection 34, 35; Hutchison Library 2, 6, 8/9, 22, 33, 37, 40, 42/43, 43 (bottom), 44, 44/45, 47; Peter Newark's American Pictures 23, 26, 32; J. Sainsbury Ltd 43 (top); Spanish Tourist Board 39; Zefa Picture Library 38/39, 41.

Contents

TRADING AND TRADERS

Every time you go into a store and buy something, you are taking part in trade. Trade is buying and selling. It is the exchange of goods and services that has gone on since prehistoric times and is now a global activity that affects us all.

Above: Shopping is something that most people do frequently. In Western countries, shopping often means a visit to a big city store, though there are still many small shops like this one.

Right: For many people in the developing countries of Africa and Asia, shopping usually means a trip to the local street market.

When you buy something, you can almost guarantee that it has changed hands (and shape) many times before it reaches you. This book, for instance, was written by the author and sold to the publisher. The publisher edited it and acquired the pictures for it. Then it was printed—perhaps in a different country—and shipped to the company's warehouse. The company's sales force then sold copies of the book to school and public libraries. Another edition may have been sold to bookstores, or retailers, by the sales force or by wholesalers. The retailers sold the book to a consumer. You, the consumer, may have purchased this book in a bookstore or found it in a library.

Domestic trade

Trade that takes place within one country is called domestic trade. Some manufacturers sell their products direct to their customers or to retailers, but most find it more efficient to sell to a wholesaler. A wholesaler buys and stores goods in large quantities. A book wholesaler would, for instance, stock books from almost all the publishers in the country. Retailers buy small quantities of many books from the wholesaler. The retailer might be a small shop or a large department store.

International trade

Few countries in the world can produce all the food and products that they need or want. Countries import goods, food, and raw materials from other countries. They try to export what they can produce in greater quantity.

Foreign trade is complicated because many different currencies are involved. Banks and other financial institutions organize the exchange of currency. The rates of exchange depend on the supply of and demand for the currency, which in turn depends on the supply of and demand for the country's products.

The first traders had no money. Today money itself is bought and sold. The most influential markets in the world are the international markets, dealing in currency, stocks and bonds, shares, and valuable commodities (trade items) such as gold and oil. Vast sums of money change hands every day in these markets.

Trading communities

Most Western countries believe in free trade. In a capitalist free market the consumer's demand for a particular product determines its supply and its price. Some nations attempt to regulate the price of goods and restrict imports by taxing foreign goods or limiting the amount that may be imported. Other nations encourage trade by removing customs duties among themselves and imposing tariffs on the goods of countries outside their trading community. In China and formerly in Russia the government controlled the price of goods and their distribution. This communist system failed, and most communist nations are now introducing economic reforms and changing to free market economies.

Above: The Tokyo stock exchange. In one day's trading on the stock exchange, the value of a company may rise or fall by millions.

THE FIRST TRADERS

The first humans were wandering hunters with no permanent homes. They relied on themselves for everything—food, clothes, and shelter. Then they realized that they could have more good things if they traded with each other.

About 10,000 years ago people began to plant crops and domesticate animals. They built the first villages. Because they lived in one place, they had time to develop skills other than food gathering and hunting wild animals, which had formerly occupied all their time. They could also acquire possessions because they would not have to carry them around.

Settled communities

People began to specialize, practicing one skill until they had mastered it. Some made cloth on primitive looms. Others made clay pots for storing water and grain. The people in one village began to trade with their neighbors in the next, making trails through the forest to a meeting place where trade goods such as cloth, pots, fishhooks, and baskets could be exchanged.

One of the earliest trades was in flint. Flint is a kind of stone used to make tools. In prehistoric Europe, flint from France was traded as far as the Swiss lakes. The traders moved along the river valleys, for there were no roads and most of the land was thick with forest. Often villages were built by rivers, so rivers became trade routes.

Bartering

Before money was invented, people bartered, or exchanged, goods. Someone with four pots to sell would take a goat in exchange. He might then barter the goat

The first traders exchanged goods, using a system of barter. These people are exchanging blocks of salt for amber beads made by their neighbors.

for two sacks of grain. This still happens in some places.

Among tribal communities, people traded in whatever they had to exchange. Australian Aborigines traded in red ochre (a dye), shells, belts made from hair, boomerangs, and spears. Native North American societies traded meat, vegetables, furs, pottery, and blankets with one another. Later, Native Americans traded with the white settlers who offered new trade goods such as iron knives and pots, mirrors, and guns.

Money

Some communities introduced tokens to pay for goods in the form of shells or beads, or even ingots of metals such as copper, bronze, or iron. The ancient Egyptians valued goods in terms of copper weights, but they never thought of using them as coins. The first people to use money (about 2,600 years ago) may have been the Lydians, who lived in what is now Turkey. Lydian coins were thick ovals of metal stamped with a symbol showing their weight. From Lydia, the use of coins spread to Greece. But for a long time, coins were used only for big transactions. The coins were far too valuable to be used for day-to-day purchases.

It was not until the fifth century B.C. that payment in money became common. The Romans used coins, and as they colonized the known world, their coinage became international.

Money is a fairly recent invention. Before there were coins, people used tokens such as cowrie shells from the beach. Cowries are mollusks found in Africa, Asia, and Australia. The first coins we know of may have come from Lydia, but they may also have been invented in China and India even earlier.

By Land and Sea

Above: The Phoenicians traded in a dye called Tyrian purple, made from a mollusk known as a murex.

Below: Phoenician merchants wait in their ships while African traders inspect the goods and set out their own produce in exchange.

As trade developed, traders began to look beyond their own communities for customers. The people who produced the goods did not always want to spend too much time selling their produce. Their skill was in producing. So people who were good at selling did it for them and made a profit. These people who sold merchandise were called merchants.

Merchants in ancient times were adventurers as much as traders. Often they ventured into unknown lands in search of trade. As they did so, they discovered new lands and spread their culture. There were few roads, so overland travel was difficult and dangerous. The merchants traveled on foot, or by donkey or camel. Besides having to carry goods vast distances and to keep them from spoiling or being stolen, traders had no international currency and no standard weights and measures.

Traders from around the Mediterranean traveled by sea. The Phoenicians, who lived along the coast of what

is now Lebanon, became expert voyagers. Their merchants traveled in galleys between the Aegean Islands with cargoes of obsidian, a black volcanic glass that was prized for making knife blades, and cloth that was dyed a rich purple-red. Some bold Phoenicians even ventured into the stormy Atlantic Ocean and began a trade in tin with the people of Cornwall in Britain.

SALT AND SILK

Salt may not seem particularly valuable to us, but it is essential to the diet of both humans and animals, and it can be used to preserve food. In the ancient world it was highly valued. Salt is found naturally in dry regions, where water evaporates in the hot sun. Camel caravans crossing the North African deserts stopped at oases to collect sacks of salt to be traded elsewhere.

The demand for salt created trade routes. The Romans had a "salt road," the Via Salaria, along which salt was brought from the port of Ostia. This town, founded to produce salt, was originally at the mouth of the the Tiber River and was established at about the same time as Rome. It became a harbor for merchant ships and later an important trading center.

The brotherhood of trade

Like any other ancient city, Ostia had a market where food and other goods were bought and sold, or exchanged. There were stands selling fresh produce from the countryside alongside permanent stores that sold bread, meat, wine, groceries, pots, and other goods.

Every trade had its own trade organization, or guild. The builders met for dinners; the bakers met to elect a president for the year; the butchers drew up regulations for the running of the meat trade within the town. Eventually these trade guilds became very important in town life.

The Silk Road

Silk was one of the most valuable trade goods in the ancient world. The Romans loved to wear brightly colored silks, but they had to pay high prices for this luxury. Silk was made only in China from the delicate threads spun by the caterpillar of the silk moth. Only the Chinese knew how to raise silkworms, and they guarded the secret jealously. More than 2,000 years ago, Persian merchants from what is now Iran made the long journey to buy silk from the Chinese, and they carried their precious goods back westward along an overland route that became famous as the Silk Road. Damascus in Syria was the meeting place for East and West, where Chinese silk was sold to traders from Rome.

The Roman port of Ostia was a rich, bustling place. Its shopping streets were full of market traders and merchants from all over the Mediterranean world.

14

PINCHES OF SALT

Salt has been a valuable substance throughout history. In parts of Africa, small bags of salt were used as money. An Arab host showed his courtesy by sharing salt with his guest.

Roman soldiers were paid money to buy their own salt; from their Latin word *salarium* comes our word salary. People still say that people are "not worth their salt" if they do not do a good day's work.

THREADS OF SILK

Persia controlled the rich silk trade until A.D. 550. Then, as the story goes, two monks from the West smuggled silkworm eggs out of China hidden inside bamboo canes.

The Arabs brought silkworms to Europe in the A.D. 800s. Later, Italy and France developed silk-weaving industries. In the 1500s immigrants from the Low Countries (Belgium and Holland) took their weaving skills to England and started the silk industry there. Later, American settlers set up properous silk factories in Connecticut and New Jersey.

THE MIDDLE AGES

After the fall of the Roman Empire, many areas of Europe were threatened by barbarian tribes, who sacked fine cities and caused tremendous upheavals. Patterns of trade were disrupted and travel, which had become much safer, became perilous once again.

Most people in Europe continued to live as farmers in self-contained communities, but gradually more and more began to live in towns. The towns were mostly well-defended administrative centers built on coasts or rivers. Traders preferred to move their goods by water because the roads were so bad.

During the Middle Ages, however, many inventions and discoveries made travel easier. New shipbuilding techniques helped make ships easier to steer and sail

A camel caravan wends its way across the desert. Trade goods passed to and from Europe and Asia across the barren lands of the Middle East. Traveling in a group gave the merchants protection against robbers.

into the wind. The stirrup, horseshoe, and padded horse collar were invented. These enabled horses to pull much heavier loads and their riders to stand in the saddle and fight off attackers if the need arose.

The Byzantine Empire and Islam

The Byzantine Empire (the eastern half of the old Roman Empire) was rich in agricultural land. Its traders sold grain grown in North Africa and around the Mediterranean. They sold wine, olives, and olive oil from Greece, as well as meat, fish, and dried fruits. From the Near East came gold, glass, and stone. Leather, cotton, and papyrus were also valuable commodities. Byzantine merchants traded these goods for luxuries from China, India, Africa, and Russia. They imported spices, silk, precious stones, ivory, and furs. They carried the goods overland in well-guarded caravans.

In the seventh century Islam was founded, a new religion whose followers were bent on spreading their faith. They conquered more and more of the Byzantine Empire and in so doing made trading conditions safer and easier. There were no hostile borders for merchants to cross, and there was a single currency—the dinar—a gold coin used by everyone.

Trade wars

Western Europe was still Christian and determined to stay that way. From the eleventh century to the thirteenth century, European monarchs conducted wars called Crusades in an attempt to regain control of the Holy Land to which they believed they had sole right. The crusaders traveled east through the Italian cities of Pisa, Genoa, and Venice. They stocked up there with weapons and supplies for the rest of the journey and paid for them in goods brought back from the East. As a result these cities grew immensely rich.

Venice above all prospered by transporting the crusaders to the Holy Land by ship and setting up trading posts there. The returning ships brought ginger, peppercorns, cinnamon, cloves, and other spices that the wealthy craved, together with sweet exotic fruits, such as peaches and dates. They brought beautiful rugs, silks, and jewels that were highly prized. The Venetian merchants could hardly meet the demand for luxuries.

THE FEUDAL SYSTEM

The feudal system dominated life in the Middle Ages. Peasants who worked on the land had little freedom. They owed allegiance to the lord who owned their land. The lord, in his turn, owed allegiance to a greater lord or directly to the king. He had to provide knights and fighting men to fight the king's wars. Peasants had to give part of their labor and most of what they grew to the lord's estate.

In the 1300s a plague known as the Black Death swept across Europe. Thousands of people died. Afterward, there were so few peasants that they could demand freedom, and the feudal system gradually disappeared.

FAIRS AND FAIR TRADE

Throughout the Middle Ages, isolated farming communities produced virtually everything they needed. To them people from the next village were foreign. A visit from a peddler was an exciting event, especially for the children. The peddler was a seller of trinkets and jewelry, oddities like ribbons, ornaments, and pins, and homemade medicines.

For bigger purchases and to sell surplus produce of their own, the country people had to go to the market in the nearest town. The market was in the center of the town. Around it there were narrow streets of small shops with signs outside showing what was sold inside. People working in one trade or selling the same goods tended to work on the same street. As towns grew, whole districts became devoted to one particular trade.

In a large town, market day would be once a month or even once a week. If there was no regular market, the country people waited until there was a fair.

Going to the fair

Fairs were often held on a religious holiday, such as Easter. The emperor Charlemagne, who ruled much of Europe from A.D. 800 to 814, encouraged fairs as a way of bringing people together for peaceful commerce. At the fair, local merchants enforced laws concerning fair trading and standard weights and measures. Special courts were set up to handle disputes.

Country people drove their farm animals and carried their produce long distances. Several families would set off together for company and safety. Often they had to stay overnight in an inn or in the open. By sunrise, the muddy lanes leading to town would be crowded with sheep, geese, cattle, and pigs, often driven by children.

At the market, craftsmen such as cobblers (shoemakers) and tinkers (pot menders) would do a brisk business. There were stands selling everything from ale to yarn. Storekeepers sold fruit, nuts, bread, and beer to the weary travelers. Every inn would be full, with many visitors sleeping in barns or haylofts.

The poor people gaped at the sight of richly dressed merchants and nobles parading through the streets. Crowds gathered to see the many entertainers: fortune-tellers, fire-eaters, minstrels, musicians, acrobats, dancing bears, and quack doctors selling "cures" for every imaginable illness. There were sports, too, such as wrestling and archery. Small local fairs might last for only a few days. But some bigger fairs lasted as long as seven weeks. Traders from many countries met at them to do business.

The business of banking

Banking began in northern Italy in the 1100s. At this time, Europeans used only metal coins. The Italian traveler Marco Polo was astonished to see the Chinese using paper money when he visited China in the 1270s. No merchant wanted to risk carrying large amounts of gold coins for fear of being robbed. So merchants made arrangements with goldsmiths. The goldsmiths held gold for the merchants in a safe place. When a merchant wanted to buy something, he handed over to the seller a note, telling the goldsmith to pay the bearer of the note the correct sum in gold. The goldsmith had become a banker and charged the merchants a fee for his services.

Market day in medieval Europe brought country people, and their animals, to town. Ale sellers, peddlers, cake sellers, and quack doctors cried their wares. Goldsmiths offered the first banking service to traders.

19

CITIES AND GUILDS

The Vikings who lived in what is now Scandinavia were the most important traders in northern Europe during the early Middle Ages. Because they were so fierce, they often took what they wanted from the peoples of western Europe, but they also traveled east to what is now Russia. They settled there and collected furs, amber, tar, and wax, as well as slaves. They sold them and the goods for luxuries brought from the Far East and China by traders.

The Hanseatic League

Later, German settlers founded wealthy towns in northern Europe and took over most of the trade. But their merchants were threatened by robbers on land and pirates at sea. To counter this threat, several towns banded together to give each other mutual support and protection. These trading associations were known as "hanse." Eventually merchants of some 90 towns or more in northern Europe joined this Hanseatic League. They controlled trade in the Baltic and neighboring seas. They ran the fur trade with Russia. The league fixed prices, hunted pirates, and kept out rival traders.

Guilds

Business in medieval times was dominated by guilds. In small towns the guild might simply be an association of all the merchants. But in larger towns guilds were more specialized. Craft guilds were formed for most of the different trades—goldsmiths, stonemasons, leather workers, carpenters, fish dealers, butchers, bakers, candlestick makers, among others. The combined wealth of the guild members made them a great power in the land. Even the king often had to ask the rich merchants for money to pay for his wars.

The guilds made rules about the way in which people worked and for how long. They controlled prices and set minumum and maximum wages for workers. They set standards of good workmanship and punished members who broke the rules. A baker caught selling a loaf of bread lighter than regulation weight was dragged through the streets wearing a fool's cap with his loaves tied around his neck.

Thanks to its trade with the East, Venice was the richest city in Europe by the fifteenth century. Earlier, Marco Polo had set out on his journey to China in 1253. He is said to have brought back the art of making ice cream and pasta (noodles in China).

Entry to the trades was controlled by the apprenticeship system. Parents would pay a fee for a son to become apprenticed to a craftsman. For up to ten years, while he learned the craft, the apprentice would receive little more than his board and lodging. At the end of his apprenticeship, he would have to demonstrate his skills to the guild in order to be admitted as a craftsman. Eventually a craftsman might become a master. Master craftsmen were important people in the guild and in the town as well.

Traveling people

In the Middle Ages travelers were marvelled at by ordinary people. Apart from merchants, pilgrims, crusaders, and nomadic herdsmen, few people took to the road or water. One group of people, however, spent all their lives traveling, and many of their descendants still do. They are often called gypsies, although they prefer to be called simply travelers.

STREET NAMES

In an old city you can still find sections devoted to one particular trade: a garment district, for example, with lots of small workshops in which workers design and make clothes.

Street names in medieval European cities often reveal the trade that was once carried on there. A famous London street is called Haymarket because hay was once sold there. Other streets include Bread Street, Poultry, and Cornhill. Close by Poultry was Scalding Alley, where chickens were made ready for the table.

TRAVELING PEOPLE

The ancestors of the traveling people came from India, arriving in Europe in the Middle Ages. They made their living by making pots and by buying and selling all kinds of goods. Going from village to village, they entertained the villagers and brought them news. They danced and performed acrobatics and told stories, but they would never settle down.

They traveled on foot or by horse and slept in tents. In the

BEFORE COLUMBUS

There is little written evidence of how trade developed in the Americas. In South and Central America the Incas and Aztecs built great empires that were pillaged and devastated by Spanish conquerors in the 1500s. The Incas lived in a society totally controlled by the ruling family. There was no opportunity for people to trade with each other, for the rulers owned everything. Families were apportioned land and had to give three-quarters of their produce to feed the nobles, priests, the army, and the poor. Though they lacked freedom, the people lived well.

Traders in gold and feathers

The Aztecs ruled an empire in Central America. Their capital city Tenochtitlán was famed for its wealth. In its market, people could exchange food, clothing, animal skins, feathers from exotic birds, pottery, tools, ornaments of gold and silver, and jewelry set with precious stones.

The ordinary village people could afford only the bare necessities of life, but village chiefs, government officials, priests, army officers, and others of high social rank had plenty of luxuries. A highly prized foodstuff was the cacao bean from which they made chocolate to drink. Another luxury was latex from the rubber trees that grew

Above left: A Turkish family of gypsies on the road. Their home and all their possessions are packed on the horse-drawn cart.

Below right: A wampum belt made by the Huron Indians. A single belt contained hundreds of tiny shell beads.

WAMPUM

Wampum was more than money. Each bead, and the color of each bead, had significance. Dark beads were prized more than white ones, though white beads stood for health, wealth, and happiness, and black or purple ones for the expression of sorrow. When the Indians made a treaty with the colonists they gave them wampum as a sign of good faith. The colonists often did not even give good faith in return.

1800s, they built wooden wagons in which they could live and travel. Today they travel in campers, trailers, and trucks. Some still speak their own Romany language.

Traveling people earn their living in a variety of ways. Some are experts in the scrap metal trade. Others sell goods they make, such as paper flowers, lace, baskets, and lucky charms. Some work in fairs and circuses. Some are migrant farm workers. A few have become well-to-do business people.

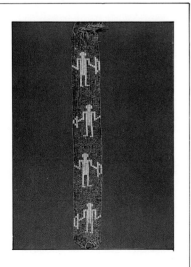

wild in the forests. The Native Americans used it to make balls to play with.

North American traders

The Aztecs and later inhabitants of Central America traded with the peoples who lived farther north. The people there loved the bright feathers of the macaw and the long tail feathers of the quetzal. They also loved golden jewelry and precious stones. They used shells as money, though how many shells it took to purchase an emerald bracelet nobody knows. For most people pottery and tools were the only goods that they could trade in exchange for food.

How the rich lived

Native Americans of the northwest coast had such a natural wealth of food from the sea and from the land that they traded very little. They built beautiful wooden homes with elaborate totem poles outside. Instead of trading with neighboring tribes, they gave their goods away in a ceremony called a potlatch. Visiting chiefs were simply invited to take a selection of goods.

Furs

In the forests and on the plains Native Americans hunted beaver and buffalo. They ate the meat and used the skins to clothe themselves and make their homes. They exchanged furs and hides with each other. When the Europeans arrived, they too were eager to trade in skins but gave the Indians mostly valueless items in exchange.

Wampum

The Native Americans of the Northeast used wampum as money. These were beads made from shells strung together. Often they were made into belts or other items of decoration that the owners wore with pride. When the first European colonists arrived, they set a standard for trading with the Indians by establishing how much wampum equaled a shilling. Eventually corrupt settlers flooded the market with so much bogus wampum that wampum lost its value. By the 1700s, most trade was carried out with real money, though it was not until 1792 that the dollar became the official monetary unit of the United States.

EXPLORING NEW WORLDS

During the 1400s, many explorers risked their lives, and lost them, in an attempt to find new trade routes to the East. Those who succeeded in their search found more than they bargained for.

Great changes took place in the world in the 1400s. The Black Death had devastated the populations of western Europe, and in the East the Byzantine Empire was finally overrun by Turks of the Ottoman Empire. They were hostile to Western merchants and closed overland trade routes to the East. There was no shortage of demand for luxury goods, so merchants were anxious to find new trade routes.

There was great rivalry among European nations to wrest control of trade from the northern Italian cities. Printing was invented, and knowledge and the desire for more knowledge spread rapidly. There were great improvements in shipbuilding. Ships were made larger and more seaworthy, able to carry great cargoes of silks, spices, and other goods from the "Indies"—China, Indonesia, and India—if only a sea route could be found.

The great expansion

In the wake of the great explorers came merchants, who set up trading posts that eventually turned into colonies controlled by these nations. The Spanish and Portuguese exploited the wealth of South America, while Britain, France, and other European nations vied with each other for trade in North America, India, and Southeast Asia.

Each nation set up trading companies. Their trading posts grew into settlements. The settlers had to make their own decisions and take care of themselves. Europe was far away, and even on a fast ship a letter from home

---

FINDING THE INDIES

The search for new routes led the Portugese to travel eastward to explore the coast of Africa, where they traded with the great Benin Empire. Vasco da Gama sailed on from Africa all the way to the coast of India.

Meanwhile Christopher Columbus, sailing west under the Spanish flag, had reached the Caribbean in 1492 and found what he thought must be India. But he had brought back no riches to tempt the Portuguese from their eastward course. Others who followed Columbus, however, did find riches. The Spanish found gold in Central and South America, and Vespucci and others, landing in North America, at last realized that Columbus had discovered a whole "New World."

In 1519 Magellan, still searching for a westward route to the Indies, sailed across the Pacific Ocean. He was killed in the Philippines, but his ships traveled on, loaded with spices. In 1522 one reached home. It was the first ship to sail completely around the world.

took weeks to arrive. Traders became governors, soldiers, and civil servants. By the early 1800s, the British East India Company was so powerful that it had won a vast Indian empire for Britain. The settlers in North America had fought for and won complete independence from Britain.

The East India Company

Traders from Britain, Holland, France, and Denmark all set up East India companies in order to trade with India and reduce Portugal's virtual monopoly. The British company made trading and administrative agreements with local rulers, and it effectively fought off competition

A European map of the known world in 1450 contained many blank spaces. Much of the Earth was simply *terra incognita*— unknown land. No traders or explorers had ventured there and returned to tell the tale.

Columbus believed that his three ships would reach Asia by sailing west across the Atlantic. He did not know about America which for him was a "New World."

The slave trade was one side
of a terrible triangular trade.
In the West Indies and Louisiana,
the colonists grew cotton and
sugarcane, which could be
made into molasses and rum,
which were much in demand
in Europe and elsewhere.
Ships from the northern
colonies brought the raw
sugar or molasses back to
New England, made it into
rum, and sailed to Africa.
There they traded the liquor for
people. They "bought" slaves
and brought them back in chains
to work, mostly under wretched

Traders at a Hudson's Bay
Company fur trading post
during the 1800s. Trappers
brought in the furs of beavers,
muskrats, and other animals,
which they caught as they
traveled in canoes along
the rivers.

OCEAN TRADERS

When European seamen first
explored the Pacific Ocean
500 years ago, they found coastal
trade flourishing. The Pacific
Ocean is dotted with thousands
of islands. Traders in small
craft were the only means of
communication between these
island communities before the
modern age brought airplanes,
radios, and telephones.

from other countries. They traded in tea (introduced
from China), cotton, and spices and controlled virtually
the whole country. In 1858 the British government
"purchased" India from the East India Company.

Traders and trappers

The first settlers in America were quickly followed by
traders. Companies were given charters by their govern-
ments to trade with the native population and with the
settlers who came from Europe to this promising New
World. Life was tough for the early settlers. Everything
they could not make had to be imported by ship from

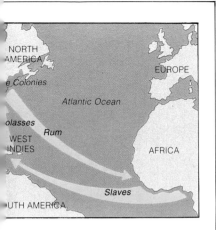

NORTH AMERICA

e Colonies

Atlantic Ocean

olasses

Rum

WEST INDIES

AFRICA

EUROPE

Slaves

UTH AMERICA

conditions on plantations producing more cotton and more sugar. This dreadful trade continued until the 1800s.

Europe. Once they were settled, they began to farm the new lands and had produce of their own to export.

The colonists built fine ships from the timber they found. They exported the timber from the forests, fish from the sea, and furs from the animals they caught. They cleared land and grew wheat, rice, potatoes, sugar, cocoa, tobacco, and hemp.

In the British colonies trade was strictly governed by Parliament which was far away in England. The colonists were allowed to produce only those goods that would be of benefit to Britain. They could not hope to sell produce, such as wheat, that would compete with wheat grown in Britain. Nor were they allowed to sell their goods to other nations.

The colonists, of course, defied the British. In their own vessels they shipped meat, fish, and farm produce to southern European ports. They exchanged these

THE MOUNTAIN MEN

As settlers moved farther west across America in the early 1800s, trading companies found that they needed ever more furs to supply the demand from Europe. They hired trappers who roamed the wild Rocky Mountains. The trappers were called mountain men. They lived in wooden cabins that they built themselves, far from the nearest settlement. Through the winter, when snow covered the forest trails, the trapper might never see another person, except perhaps a passing Native American hunter. It was a tough, lonely life.

The trappers met every year at gatherings, or rendezvous. They came into camp from the mountains to sell their furs and to buy food and other supplies for the next year. The fur company buyers came to the rendezvous to buy the furs. For the trappers, this yearly gathering was a rare chance to meet friends. They feasted on steaks, drank whiskey, sang, and danced. They loved to tell tall stories—boasting, for example, of the huge grizzly bears they had killed with their bare hands!

The Bugis people traded among the islands of Indonesia. They would unload a cargo of nutmeg at one island and buy shells or palm oil as cargo for the next stage of the voyage. They also carried news of the outside world to the islands.

Bugis traders still travel between the islands today. They build their own boats. These traditional two-masted sailing craft are called *prahus*.

for wine and fruit that Britain could not produce, sold them at a profit, and returned with ships laden with manufactured goods.

The Hudson's Bay Company

The Hudson's Bay Company was granted a charter by the British government for trading rights in the whole Hudson Bay area. The agents of the company set up trading posts where they bartered goods with the Native Americans. In exchange for beads, woolen cloth, liquor, guns, and worthless trinkets, the Indians gave them valuable furs that could be sold at a great profit in

Europe. The company's agents sent men to explore new territory and bring back more furs. They traveled by canoe along the rivers and learned from the Indians how to trap beaver and other animals and follow trails through the forests. The Native Americans were not always friendly, so the fur trappers had to be courageous.

The Hudson's Bay Company was supposed to establish settlements farther inland, but it encountered hostility from the Indians and was beset by competition from French settlers and others who disputed its right to a monopoly. There was, however, enough profit for everyone—except for the Native Americans—and several companies traded in furs. Eventually the British government bought back the land and trading rights. But by then, the company was a huge and successful business, which it remains to this day.

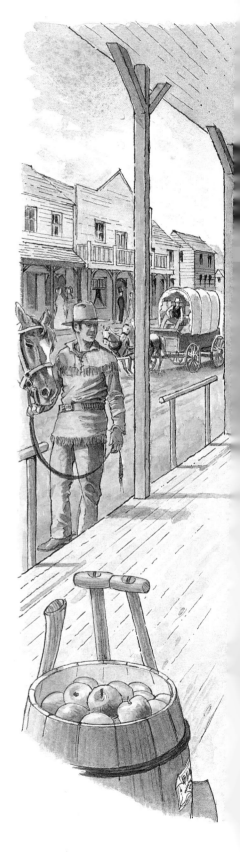

New towns

Many new settlements in America began as trading posts where Native Americans and whites met to trade furs. Later, farmers came to clear the forest and plow the land, and the trading post became a small town. Its most important building was the general store, which became the focus of community life, much like the village store in European farming communities.

The store

The storekeeper in a pioneer town sold everything the settlers might need: flour, salt, beans, and other foods; cloth to make clothes, pots and pans, farm tools, and seeds. All the goods had to be shipped in by wagon, sometimes from the distant cities of the eastern United States. People setting up new homes in the West had little in the way of luxuries. They even made their own furniture. The storekeeper could order goods from the East, "as fine as any in the great houses of Chicago." A family might wait months in great anxiety for the arrival of precious tableware or furnishings, trundled across the prairie in a wagon.

Families living in remote farms traveled into town to buy supplies at the store and hear the latest gossip. While the storekeeper made up their order, he passed on news of other families who had come in the day or the week before.

A frontier store was the center of community life. The storekeeper sold anything and everything. People came in to gaze at the crowded shelves, to buy supplies, to collect orders brought west by wagon or railroad, or simply to talk and find out what was new in the world.

THE AGE OF INDUSTRY

The invention of power-driven machines that could produce large quantities of goods led to a great expansion of trade beginning in the early 1800s. Industrial nations produced far more goods than they could consume, and they exported goods all around the world.

It was coal that fueled the Industrial Revolution. The introduction of the coal-fired blast furnace in 1760 enabled iron to be mass-produced. Coal was important, too, in the development of steam power. Steam was used to drive the new spinning machines and looms in the textile industry. Countries such as Britain that were rich in coal and iron and had a plentiful supply of imported cotton for their mills grew rich.

Britain exported more coal and iron than the rest of the world combined. A third of the world's industrial output came from Britain. By 1850, a quarter of the world's trade passed through British ports.

The movement of goods

Heavy goods, such as coal and iron, are difficult and expensive to move by road. It takes less effort to move heavy goods by boat, but rivers do not always go where the goods are needed and can carry boats only for part of their course. In the 1700s engineers in North America and Europe dug canals so boats and barges could carry timber, coal, and other heavy goods to factories. The railroads put an end to most commercial barge traffic, and the later invention of the automobile made road transportation cheaper and more efficient, but big barges still carry cargoes along the waterways of North America, Europe, and China.

From the ports heavy industrial goods could be

carried to every corner of the world by the new steamships that could cross oceans in a fraction of the time it took a sailing ship. Today cargo planes also play a role in distributing goods around the world.

The railroad

In America frontier towns grew rapidly with the coming of the railroad. Goods and people could be transported

The new factory age brought more and cheaper goods. But it meant hardship, low pay, and often dangerous conditions for many factory workers, including children.

cheaply and speedily. As a result the general store moved into larger premises made of brick rather than of rough-cut timber or adobe (dried mud). Along the street sprang up a church and a school, a blacksmith's shop, and a livery stable for stabling horses. The town might soon boast a hotel and a barbershop where dusty trail riders could get a shave and a bath before heading for the town saloon. With the coming of the automobile in the early 1900s, the frontier age was over in America. But in many small town communities the store retained its importance as a center of a town's social life, a place to chat as well as to buy.

Immigrants

Immigrants arriving in a new country often work with tireless determination to establish themselves. In the late 1800s and early 1900s, the streets of New York, Chicago,

Above: A tug towing a line of barges on a Chinese waterway. Canals are ideal for moving heavy cargoes where speed is not essential.

Left: Traders founded and built frontier towns like Helena, Montana, pictured here in 1870. Goods arrived by train and were transported onward by wagon.

and other United States cities were crowded with people who had come to America by boat from Europe and Asia with the hope of a better life.

In a new world that was very different from their homelands, the immigrants had to find a place to live and a way to earn money. Most had to learn a new language and a new way of life. Some were lucky and found jobs. A few had skills to sell, such as watch repairing, and were able to start small businesses. Many turned their

CANALS

Canals were dug in China hundreds of years ago. The Chinese invented the canal lock and were justifiably proud of their waterways. American and European canal building really gathered speed in the 1700s to

hands to whatever they could find. Because they could not afford to buy a store, they traded in the city streets. They sold matches, old clothes, or anything they could make or buy for a few pennies.

Modern immigrants, including many Asians settling in North America, Australia, and Europe, have flourished in businesses. They run restaurants and stores that often stay open until late at night. It is hard work, but the immigrants are working for their futures. Close family ties help them feel more at home in their new country.

Trust and trade

In the early days, trade was conducted in local markets, at trading posts, or at fairs. As trade developed and huge quantities of goods were involved, exchanges were set up. At first goods continued to be brought to the exchange.

Right: Immigrants tend to stick together in a new country. They bring with them their own way of life and often work very hard to establish their businesses, like this fish store in New York's Chinatown.

carry raw materials such as coal to the new factories.

The Erie Canal from Albany to Buffalo, New York, connected the Atlantic coast with the Great Lakes. It was completed in 1825.

In 1914 the Panama Canal opened. The canal linked the Atlantic and Pacific oceans.

Buyers could look at the goods and fix a price. Later, goods were bought and sold without ever being seen by the dealers. Goods were "graded" so that the customer knew what quality to expect. Shares in companies, such as shipping lines and coal mines, were bought and sold in the same way.

Banking and business developed codes of honor based on trust. Merchants were expected to pay their bills and to keep their word. Bankers were expected to

Left: For many immigrants the United States offered a world of opportunity. Then, in the 1930s came the Great Depression. Many people fell on hard times. This Tennessee family lived in a shack wallpapered with newspapers full of advertisements for goods they could not dream of buying.

Right: After Germany's defeat in World War I (1914–1918), its economy collapsed. German money became worthless. Banknotes were simply thrown away. These children, photographed in 1923, are playing with money that could buy nothing.

RUSSIA'S REVOLUTION

Russia, like all the former Soviet republics, had a communist trading system. All factories were state run. Central government set production targets. Prices were kept artificially low. Unfortunately, although the Soviet Union was good at building military equipment and spacecraft, its factories and farms failed to deliver enough consumer goods and fresh food to the stores. Russian shoppers now hope for more goods and better stores. But they also face much higher prices, and many items are still unavailable, unless bought on the flourishing black market.

be honest. In many small communities, the bank became the center of business life. The banker made loans to farmers when times were hard and looked after the savings of townspeople.

The New World

As the population of the United States expanded, so did its production and trade. By 1900, the United States was the most advanced industrial nation in the world, with massive exports of wheat, beef, iron and steel, and newly found oil. Russia, too, was rich in oil, but it was a backward country. A revolution in 1917 brought the communists to power. From then until the late 1980s agriculture and industry were rigidly controlled by the government. Today, after the dissolution of communist power, Russia and the other former Soviet republics struggle to feed their populations and bring their industries up to date.

Under the Soviet regime, there was full employment. Now many workers are being laid off so that factories can increase their productivity in order to compete with Western businesses. Unemployment is a serious problem in many capitalist countries, too.

World in turmoil

The first half of the twentieth century was a turbulent period for the whole world. Two great wars were fought, and in the years between every industrial nation suffered as a result of the Great Depression. In 1945 Europe and Japan were largely in ruins. Today Europe is prosperous again thanks to its Common Market and help from the U.S., and Japan is an economic superpower. After years of cold war hostility, the two postwar superpowers—the United States and the former Soviet Union—have begun to cooperate as the latter embraces democracy and moves toward a free-market economy.

The Great Depression

In October 1929 the booming New York stock market suddenly crashed. America had been extremely prosperous. Millions of people were able to buy cars, refrigerators, and many other consumer goods that poor people once only dreamed of owning. Factories churned out the goods and the profits. Investors rushed to buy their shares. They noticed too late that the market was flooded, and the people had spent all their money.

Companies were loaded with goods they could no longer sell. There was no point producing more, so they reduced production and laid off workers. Worried investors began to sell their shares, and the prices began to drop. Other investors panicked, and there was a great rush to sell shares before they became worthless. Companies and banks who had loaned money to investors went broke. Wages fell, and soon 12 million people were out of work.

As the United States struggled to right itself, it had to stop imports from other countries and loans to them. Unable to sell their goods, these trading nations also fell into depression.

The dictators

Some European nations, Germany particularly, suffered terrible inflation in the 1920s. People's money became worthless. They lost their savings and often their jobs as well. They blamed the government and turned to a dictator to lead them out of trouble. But Adolf Hitler, in whom so many mistakenly put their trust, led them into a terrible war that tore the world apart.

TRADING TODAY

Today's technological revolution has speeded up communications so dramatically that trade is carried on around the globe day and night by people who never meet. Money, in the form of cash, is almost a thing of the past.

Below left: Another Japanese car on the assembly line. The Japanese sell more cars than anyone else. They make cars more efficiently than other nations.

After World War II, the United States, prosperous once more, came to Europe's aid. Its Marshall Plan gave millions of dollars to the Organization for European Economic Cooperation to distribute among the war-damaged nations. Six European nations—France, Germany, Italy, Belgium, the Netherlands, and Luxembourg—formed the European Economic Community, or Common Market. With a common agricultural policy, common duties on imports, and free movement of goods, money, and people, the community thrived. Eventually Britain and other nations negotiated to join.

Postwar miracles

Germany's recovery was remarkable. With help from the United States, and tremendous hard work, the people rebuilt their cities and their industries. Their factories

Below right: Asian car making on a different scale. In Hong Kong, some children work to assemble toys for children in other countries to play with.

Below: Hong Kong returns to China's control in 1997. People wonder what will happen then to its frantic wheeling and dealing and thriving capitalist economy.

were equipped with the latest machines. They produced high-quality goods of excellent design, and their selling methods were thoroughly effective.

Japan, similarly devastated at the end of World War II, also staged a miracle recovery. Since the 1960s, Japan has dominated world trade, outshining even the United States in exports. The label "Made in Japan" is found on cars, cameras, computers, motorcycles, microwave ovens, CD players, and watches.

Japan is a land of factories. Almost all of Japan's 121 million people live in crowded towns and cities, usually in small apartments. Many Japanese have jobs connected with trade. Workers are very loyal and often stay with the same employer from school to retirement. Couples can even get married in the factory. People think of the company as a huge family and work hard for it. To many Japanese factory workers, the money they earn is less important than the pride they feel in working for a successful company. Often they forego the vacation to which they are entitled.

A family business

Increasingly other Asian countries, such as Hong Kong and South Korea, are matching Japan in trading success. The people of Hong Kong, an island off mainland China, are famous for their skills as merchants, bankers, and manufacturers. In addition to banks in skyscraper office buildings and modern electronic factories, Hong Kong has many small, family-run companies. These businesses can often be found in tiny workshops in narrow side streets. Parents, uncles, aunts, children, and grandparents all work together. They assemble car radios. They make plastic toys. They make furniture from cane. They sew garments such as jeans and T-shirts. They even print books.

Hong Kong goods are cheap to buy because the people who make them work for low wages. They work long hours, often without a day off. Some workshops employ children, although it is against the law for children under fifteen to do factory work, even in their spare time. With labor costs so low, Asian businesses are able to undercut businesses in the West. Unable to compete, many Western industries are struggling to survive.

PRODUCER TO CONSUMER

Wherever goods are made, raw materials have to be transported to the factory and the finished products distributed to the customers. With traders selling their products worldwide, this is often a very complex and expensive business. This book, for instance, was printed in Europe and carried by ship to a port in the United States. From there, it traveled by truck to a bindery where the cover was put on and from there by truck to the publisher's warehouse. Meanwhile, the company had to make possible customers aware of the book's existence and make it attractive to them so it could be sold.

Selling the goods

Traders everywhere want their goods to reach as many customers as possible. Companies do this by marketing their products. One important aspect of marketing is advertising. Many companies spend millions of dollars advertising in newspapers and magazines, on billboards, and on television. Without advertising, few products sell in great quantity.

Companies also strive to make their products attractive to customers. They spend money on market research, finding out what the customers want by way of questionnaires and studying patterns of past sales. They

of countries during that time, so they save a lot of time and money. Businesses of every kind, including boat builders, engineers, computer firms, food processers, car manufacturers, and book publishers—get together for trade fairs. World fairs that show the best products from countries all around the world in one place rival the Olympic Games in size and cost.

have to make sure that the design of their products combines high quality with a look that appeals to customers. They have to package their goods so the customer will be drawn to them rather than to rival products.

The sales force

The larger the company, generally the more salespeople it will have on the road. The salespeople are the company's personal contact with the customer. Salespeople may travel locally, around the country, or around the world showing samples and taking orders from old customers, finding new customers, and making sure that all customers are satisfied with the goods they buy.

Above: Putting on a trade show for international visitors. In 1992 the world came to Seville, Spain, for Expo 92.

Left: On the move across the world's highways, trucks carry most of the goods we buy.

SHOPPING

Once city streets echoed to the cries of street traders such as the iceman, the fish peddler, and the flower seller, calling out their wares. Instead of customers visiting stores, they could stay at home and buy at the door from the street traders. Some, like the baker and the milkman, visited the street every day; others came less often. Traders pushed small pushcarts or walked alongside carts drawn by plodding horses that nuzzled in their nosebags of oats every time the cart stopped for the trader to make a sale.

Thanks to modern technology, customers can now do much of their shopping without stirring from home. They can select goods from magazines, their television screen, or computer monitors and use the telephone to buy and pay for them. Personal shopping can, however, be a pleasure, and there is little sign of its popularity waning.

The main street

In the United States, Australia, and most European countries, shopping has changed greatly since the 1930s. Before then, almost all stores were small family businesses. A small town had a main street with a selection of stores. One store sold groceries, another clothes, another hardware, and so on. People went from store to store.

Inside the store, the storekeeper and sales assistants stood behind a counter and served each customer in turn. Storekeepers took on youngsters as apprentices. An apprentice had to sweep the floor, stock the shelves, wrap the goods in brown paper, and carry them out to a waiting car, or deliver them later by bike. More often, however, people did their shopping on foot. Housewives went to the stores every day to buy fresh food. They could buy only as much as they could carry in their shopping bags.

Today people do much of their shopping in supermarkets and self-service stores. For major purchases of furniture, or electrical goods, they go to department stores, often located in a mall or shopping center. Some of these large stores and centers are situated outside town. There is a bigger selection of goods to choose from but less personal service than was offered by the old-time storekeeper.

The personal touch. A street trader offers a modest display of flowers and vegetables. Money changes hands between customer and trader.

Megashopping, big-city style.
Shoppers ride the escalators
or watch the crowds from a
restaurant table in the Trump
Tower shopping center in
New York City.

Corner stores

Small stores have not disappeared completely. Many towns still have a corner store with an astonishing variety of goods. The customers include elderly people who have little to buy and people who have no time to run to a bigger store. Often they sell items that people might have forgotten to get on their weekly shopping trip.

In the city, small stores also have a role. As office workers hurry from their trains and buses, the small stores are open and ready to do business. Newspaper stands, coffee and tobacco shops, and flower stands are open for business all day.

Wholesale markets

Supermarkets have their fresh food such as fish, fruit, and vegetables delivered. Restaurant owners and some small specialty shop owners still go to central markets to select and buy fresh produce. Fish dealers go to the fish market, butchers to the meat market, vegetable sellers to the vegetable market, florists to the flower market, and so on. Before dawn, trucks from the countryside, airport, or docks arrive at the central market such as Hunts Point in the Bronx, New York. The market traders—wholesalers—set out their wares. By dawn, the market is busy with shopkeepers and restaurateurs selecting what they want to sell in their shop or what the chef needs for today's menu. While most people are still getting up and eating breakfast, the market traders are doing business. By midmorning, their work day is done, and they will be clearing up their stands.

The people who work in the market know one another well. Many of the businesses have been in the same family for many years. Deals are done with a nod and a handshake. People who have been in the business for years have learned to trust one another.

Street markets

Some of the customers of the central market are market traders themselves on a smaller scale. Because they do not have to own or rent a shop, market and street traders can sell the produce at lower prices than ordinary stores. The customers can sometimes bargain, or haggle, with the traders to try to reduce the price to be paid.

that is, mixing in other substances. Bakers put potato flour into bread. Dishonest grocers added dust or ground-up twigs to spices.

Today government regulations and food hygiene laws protect consumers from being swindled or poisoned. Public health officials visit stores and restuarants to make sure that food is kept clean and prepared properly.

Right: Supermarket chains buy in bulk (often whole crops of fruit or vegetables from a farm). A supermarket sells a huge range of items, including perishable foods that must be delivered fresh every day.

Below: In a wholesale flower market, a prospective buyer checks the quality and price of the assorted blooms.

A typical street market. Traders start their day early, buying fruit and vegetables at the wholesale market before setting up their stands to catch the customer's eye.

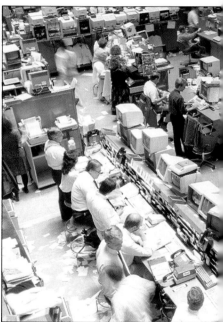

Left: African women selling their produce at market. They grow vegetables and carry them to the local town to sell. Like most markets, it is a cheerful meeting place where bargains are struck and friendships renewed.

RICH AND POOR DEALS

In many Eastern countries, especially in Arab countries, there are no price tickets on the goods. People are expected to haggle. Market traders are surprised if a visitor promptly pays the asking price. In many poor countries, buyers need to get the lowest price they can and the trader the highest, so the bargaining is in earnest.

Everything on show

In places where there are no stores, let alone department stores, everything is for sale in the market. African markets teem with things to see, smell, and admire. You may see live animals in baskets, tethered chickens, meat and fish, and an amazing variety of fruits and vegetables, herbs and spices, and medicines. There will be colorful cloth, wooden carvings and pots, clay pots and cooking utensils, jewelry, and all types of household goods.

In a Nigerian village, market day is especially busy for the women because they run the market. Most of the goods for sale are displayed in baskets on the ground. The seller sits beside them and encourages passersby to inspect them.

Million-dollar markets

A Nigerian street market is a far cry from the frantic trading floors of Wall Street, but they are linked. Often what the man in rolled-up shirtsleeves is dealing in with ears glued to the telephone and eyes to a flickering computer screen is the produce of the Nigerian village. Many poor countries grow cash crops that are sold on world markets. Instead of tending their own land and producing enough to feed the family, young Africans increasingly work on plantations.

Fair shares for all

There has been an enormous increase in world trade, but it has generally not benefited poor countries. In the 1800s cheap mass-produced goods from industrial countries flooded into the poor countries. The goods were cheaper than those produced locally by slower methods. Home industries were wiped out, just as the industries of rich countries are now threatened by goods mass-produced in Eastern countries.

In many parts of the world people are too poor to buy consumer goods at all. Many have too little food to eat and no money at all. Trade helped break down the barriers between the former communist nations of Eastern Europe and the democratic nations of the West. Trade is helping many Asian nations to grow rich. Perhaps further growth in trade will help the poorest countries of the world to feed their populations.

Traders on the floor of the San Francisco stock exchange. Theirs is a world of computer screens, fax machines, and international telephone calls. Yet a deal is a deal, wherever and however it is made.

Glossary

Adulteration The addition of inferior substances to food.

Advertising Telling people about goods for sale, through posters, magazines, and television commercials.

Agents Representatives who act on behalf of a country or company.

Amber The fossilized resin from pine trees that can be made into beads or other jewelry.

Apprenticeship Training program for young people who learn a trade from older workers.

Bargaining see *Haggle*.

Barter To trade by exchanging, or bartering, goods.

Billboards Giant outdoor signs used for posting advertisements.

Black market Unofficial trade in goods that are illegal or in short supply.

Bonds Certificates issued by a government or private company as a means of borrowing money.

Capitalist Person or country that practices an economic system based on the private ownership of capital (money and property).

Caravans Groups of merchants or travelers traveling by camel and other beasts in the East.

Cash crops Crops grown for export rather than to feed a country's own people.

Charters Official documents authorizing the activities of an organization or business.

Colonists Settlers in a new country who set up a colony that is governed by their native country.

Colony Territory governed by a foreign country, or a group of people settling in a foreign land.

Commerce Trade or business dealings.

Commodities Goods that are traded.

Common Market Another name for the European Economic Community.

Communist Person or country that practices or believes in an economic and political system in which the state controls banks, farms, and factories.

Competition Rivalry between businesses to cut costs and increase sales.

Consumer Person who buys or uses a product.

Consumer goods Goods other than food.

Currency A measure of monetary value in different countries.

Customers People who buy goods.

Customs duties Taxes on goods moving from one country to another.

Dealers Persons who sell goods or services.

Democracy Government by the people.

Department store Large store with various departments, or sections, each selling different kinds of goods.

Depression Slump in business, leading to factory closures and unemployment.

Economies Systems of managing money and business.

European Economic Community Trading and economic grouping of European nations.

Exchange To give something in return for something else.

Exchanges Places where goods or stocks are traded.

Export To sell goods abroad. Exports are goods that one country sells to another.

Fair A large annual market in the Middle Ages; today, an exhibition for businesses to display their latest products.

Feudal system Form of government, based on overlordship, which was common in the Middle Ages.

Free trade Trade between countries without customs duties on goods.

Frontier Border on a wilderness.

Galleys Ships with oars and sails used in ancient times.

Great Depression see *Depression*.

Guild Association of people in the same trade.

Haggle To bargain; buyer and seller make offers and counteroffers before agreeing on a selling price.

Immigrants People moving to live in another country.

Import To buy goods from abroad. Imports are goods bought by one country from another.

Industrial Revolution Rapid development of industry as a result of mechanization, particularly in eighteenth- and nineteeth-century Britain.

Inflation Fall in the value of money.

Investors People who put money into a business by buying shares.

Labor Workers; people employed for wages.

Lock Place on canal or river where water level can be raised or lowered to allow passage of boats.

Mall A covered shopping area with stores and restaurants that open onto a central area.

Market Place where things are bought and sold.

Marketing Planning and running a sales campaign for a product.

Market research Finding out what customers expect and want from products.

Mass-produced Made in large numbers in a factory.

Merchandise Goods for sale.

Merchants Persons who sell goods.

Monopoly Having sole control over a trade and thus being able to fix prices.

Output Goods made by factories.

Peddler Traveling seller in olden times.

Pioneer Person who goes into new territory ahead of others. Pioneer towns in America grew from pioneer settlements in the wilderness.

Pirates Sea robbers, common until the 1800s.

Plague Contagious disease.

Plantation Farm where a single crop such as bananas, tea, or cotton is grown.

Potlatch Native American ceremony in which gifts are given to guests.

Productivity Efficiency of producing goods (cheaply and quickly).

Profit Money earned from trade in excess of the costs of making and selling the goods.

Ransom Money paid for release of a prisoner.

Raw materials The ingredients factories need to make goods, such as timber, iron, and plastics.

Rendezvous Meeting of traders and trappers in colonial America.

Restaurateur Person who runs a restaurant.

Retailers Traders who sell goods direct to customers in a store.

Sales force Workers whose job it is to sell a company's products.

Samples Specimen goods shown by salesperson to prospective buyers.

Settlers People who move to a new country or region and set up a colony.

Share see *Stocks and shares*.

Shilling Unit of currency of British colonists in America. There were 20 shillings to a pound.

Shopping center A cluster of stores around a central parking area.

Silent trade Trade carried on without traders coming face to face or communicating verbally.

Standards Regulations setting quality and safety of goods on sale.

Stock market Exchange where stocks and shares are bought and sold.

Stocks and shares Pieces of paper representing goods or part of a company, sold to raise money; investors in return get the right to vote on company matters and a share of any profits.

Supermarket Large self-service store.

Surplus Goods or money left over; a farmer may have surplus crops after feeding his own family.

Tariffs Taxes on goods.

Trade fairs Meetings and exhibitions where companies show their goods and trade to one another.

Trade routes Overland, river, or sea routes used by merchants.

Trading community Group of merchants or people trading with one another.

Trading post A location or outpost, particularly in the United States, where traders bought and sold goods.

Transactions Deals.

Undercut To produce goods and sell them at a lower price than another trader.

Wampum Items made of tiny shells used as trading tokens by Native Americans.

Warehouse Building in which trade goods are stored.

Wholesalers Traders who buy from manufacturers and sell to retailers (merchants).

Index